DEAD JOKES

CW01513151

ISBN-9781724152206

A man drowned. All his friends showed up at his funeral with life jackets on. It's what he would've wanted.

Will glass coffins ever become popular? Remains to be seen.

"I had a dream last night that I was chopping vegetables with the Grim Reaper – I was dicing with death."

Buck died in a fire and his body is horrifically burned. The mortician sends for his two closest friends, Beau and Willie to identify the body.

Beau arrives first and when the mortician shows him the body, Beau says, "Gee, his face got burnt up real bad. You better turn him over." The mortician turns him over onto his front, and Beau says, "No, that ain't Buck." The mortician thinks this is highly unusual. He then brings Willie in to identify the charred remains.

Willie takes a look at the face and says, "Yup, that fire got him real good. Roll him over." The mortician rolls him over and Willie says, "Nope, that's not Buck." The mortician asks, "How can you be sure?" Willie said, "Well, you see, Buck had two assholes." "What? He had two assholes?!" says the mortician. "he sure did, every time we were out together, the townsfolk would say, 'Here's Buck with those two assholes.'"

Two men are hunting in the forest when one suddenly collapses. He is unresponsive and his eyes are glazed over. The other hunter calls an ambulance. He gasps, "I think my friend is dead! What do I do?" The dispatcher says "You need to be calm. I can help. First of all, we need to make sure he's dead." There is a long silence, then a loud gun shot is heard. The hunter then says to the dispatcher "OK, now what?"

A funeral is held for a woman who had recently passed away. While the pallbearers are carrying the casket, they accidentally bump it into a wall. They hear what sounds like a woman moan. Upon opening the casket they find that the woman is still alive. She manages to live for many more years and then passes away. Another funeral is held for her. At the end of the service, the pallbearers carry the casket out to the hearse. As they are walking, the husband screams out, "Be careful, don't hit the wall!"

Two friends are chatting in a bar. The first one asks,

"Did your hear the news, John's dead?"

"You're kidding, how did he die?"

"Well he was driving over to my house yesterday and as he pulled up outside the house his brakes failed and bang, he hit the curb, the car rolled over and he was thrown out through the sunroof, was catapulted through the air and crashed through my bedroom window."

"What a terrible way to die!" the other friend says

"Well funnily enough, that didn't kill him. So, he's lying on my floor, covered in broken glass. He tried to pull himself up by grabbing the handle of the wardrobe. He is almost on his feet when the wardrobe comes crashing down on top of him, squashing him and smashing his bones."

"What a way die, that's awful!"

"Guess what?, that didn't kill him. He very slowly managed to get the wardrobe off him and staggers out onto the landing, he attempts to balance himself against the banister but under his weight, it breaks and he falls onto to the first floor. The broken banister poles land on him, pinning him to the floor and piercing his body."

"Holey moley, what a gruesome death!"

"Well, in a surprise twist of fate that didn't kill him, he still survived. He slowly managed to crawl into the kitchen and pull himself up towards the stove but accidentally grabbed a big pot of boiling hot soup which he unwittingly poured on himself, giving him third degree burns."

"The poor guy, at least that put him out of his misery!"

"Well, he survived that! He's lying on the ground, covered in boiling hot tomato soup and he sees the phone and tries to hoist himself up to call for an ambulance, but he mistakenly grabbed the light switch and pulled the whole thing off the wall and the soup and electricity didn't mix and so he was electrocuted"

"Now that is one seriously painful way to go!"

"No, he survived that…"

"Now wait just a minute just how did he actually die?"

"Well, I shot him!"

"You shot him? Why In Gods name did you shoot him?"

"He was destroying my house."

A respectable lady walks into a pharmacy, approaches the pharmacist, looks him straight in his eyes, and says, "I would like to purchase some cyanide please." The shocked pharmacist asks, "For what possible reason could you need cyanide?" The lady replies, "Well, I want to poison my husband." The very shocked pharmacists says, "Have you lost your mind? I won't give you cyanide to murder your husband! That's morally, ethically and legally wrong plus I'll have my pharmacist license revoked! We'll end up in jail! I absolutely will not give you cyanide!" The lady calmly puts her hand in her purse and pulls out a picture of her husband and the pharmacist's wife in bed together. After looking at the photo the pharmacist replies, "That won't be a problem madam. I didn't know you had a prescription."

A cab passenger taps the driver on the shoulder to ask him a question. The cab driver freaks out, loses control of the car, almost hits a truck, mounts the footpath, and stops inches from a store front. There is a long silence in the cab, then the driver says, "Listen buddy, please don't ever

do that again. You scared the hell out of me!" The passenger apologized and says, "I didn't know you were so jumpy" The cab driver says, "It's not really your fault, you see this is my first day as a cab driver, I've been driving a hearses for the last 20 years."

I took my grandmother to a Thai massage parlor where little fish eat your dead skin for only $35. It was considerably cheaper than having a burial service.

A man is sitting at a sold out Broadway show with an empty seat beside him. During the interval a woman notices the empty seat and asks why such a valuable commodity was not occupied. The man replies that his wife was unable to attend. The woman asked him if any family members or friends could have used the seat. To which he replied, "Actually, they're all at the funeral."

There was an Englishman, a Scotsman and an Irishman working on scaffolding. The Englishman said, "Damn it, I'm sick of this, If I have egg in my sandwich tomorrow I'm going to jump off this scaffolding." The Scotsman said, "If I have peanut butter in my sandwich tomorrow, I'll jump too." The Irishman said, "I bloody hate tuna, If I have it tomorrow, I'll jump for sure." The next day, the Englishman had egg, the Irishman had tuna, and the Scotsman had peanut butter. So they all jumped to their deaths. At the funerals, the partners of the Scotsman and Englishman said, "I don't know why they didn't just tell us they wanted something else in their sandwiches?" The Irish lady said, "I don't know why my husband jumped off the off the scaffolding. He alway made his own sandwiches."

A man had died. A beautiful funeral was in progress and the priest told many great stories about the deceased, what a decent man, loving husband and wonderful father he was. The widow leaned over and whispered to her sons, "one of you take a look in the casket and make sure that's your father in there."

A very old man was lying on his death bed. His most favorite thing in the world was chocolate brownies. As he lay on his bed struggling for each breath, he thought he could smell freshly-baked brownies. He slowly got out of bed and crawled backwards down the stairs. As he suspected, there was a large platter of chocolate brownies on the kitchen table. Using all his determination, he somehow made it to the table and he reached a frail hand towards the tasty treats. NO!, his wife slapped his hand and shouted, "Leave them alone - they're for the funeral!"

A highly respected heart surgeon had died and many people attended his funeral. The casket was displayed in front of a massive heart. When the priest had finished the ceremony and after everyone had paid their respects to the family, the heart opened and the coffin rolled inside then the heart closed again.

One of the mourners burst out laughing. The guy next to him said, "show some respect man".

"I apologize", he replied, "I started thinking about my own funeral".

"What's so funny about that"?

"Well, I'm a gynecologist".

Bob came home drunk one night He fell into bed beside his wife and drifted into a deep booze induced sleep. He awoke outside the Pearly Gates, where St. Peter said, 'You are here because you died in your sleep, Bob....' Bob was shocked. 'I'm dead? No, It can't be! I've got so much left to do. I want to go home!' St. Peter said, 'I'm sorry, however there is one way you can go back, and that is as a chicken.' Bob was horrified but he agreed, he asked St. Peter to send him to a farm near his house. Moments later, he had feathers and he was clucking. A rooster walked past. 'Right, so you're the new hen in town, eh? How are things working out for you?'

'I'm not too sure,' said Bob the hen, 'but I have this weird feeling, like I'm going to burst!'

'You're probably ovulating,' said the rooster.

Surely you've laid an egg before? '

'Nope, first time,' said Bob.

'Well, just stay calm and don't fight it, it's the most natural thing in the world' said the rooster.

Bob took the Roosters advice, and after some very slight discomfort, out came an egg!

Bob was overcome with joy as he experienced motherhood for the first time. He then laid another egg and he became very emotional.

Just as he was about to pop out his third egg, he felt a slap on of his head and heard his wife shout.....

 'Bob, wake up you drunk son of a bitch.......
You've shit the bed!

My daughter's school teacher called me today.

She said, "Jane didn't show up for school this morning and I was wondering is everything alright?"

I said, "I'm afraid her mother passed away yesterday, she's still trying to deal with everything."

"The poor girl, how's she coping?" She asked.

"Extremely well," I replied. "She's just made dinner and now she's starting a second load of washing."

I was out digging a hole today when I found a box full of old gold coins.

I was so excited that and I ran to the house to show my wife...

And then It dawned on me why I was digging the hole in the first place.

My wife called me and said, "please come to the hospital. My mother hasn't got long to live!"

I replied "But the big game is on tonight". She said "Record it and watch it later."

You should have seen the surprise on her face when I arrived at the hospital with the video camera and tripod!

My dad passed away and when we didn't know his blood type. As he drew his final breath, he kept asking us to "be positive," but it's so hard without him.

A husband and his discontented wife were on holiday in Jerusalem when she died unexpectedly.

The funeral director said, "It will cost $6,000 to fly her home or $100 to bury her here in Jerusalem."

The Husband says he wants to fly her home.

The funeral director said, "But Sir, why not bury her in the holy land and save a lot of money?"

The Husband says, " Well buddy, many years ago a man named Jesus was buried here and 3 days later he rose from the dead - I'm flying her home".

Billy arrives at school at 11 o'clock.

Teacher: Billy, what have you got to say for yourself, do you know you're two hours late?

Billy: I'm sorry Miss, my Dad got burnt.

Teacher: Oh dear, I'm sorry to hear that. Is it serious?

Billy: Well, They don't joke around down at the crematorium.

I was walking down the street this morning and I saw my doctor get hit by a truck.

"Please, help me," he begged.

So I walked over and said 'I'm sorry but I'm busy right now, so I want you to take two paracetamol and if there is no improvement by the morning then phone for an appointment'.

A man goes to the doctor to get the results of his blood test. The doctor says,

"Mr Jones, do you want the good news or the bad news first?"

"Let me know the bad news please Doctor" he replies."

"Right then, you've only got 48 hours to live." Says the doctor. The man is shaken and asks,

"Well, what's the good new then?" The doctor replies,

"We are going to name a disease after you."

DEAD JOKES

I went to my sisters funeral yesterday. She died after being struck on the head with a tennis ball.

It was a beautiful service.

John had a massive heart attack and died, $35,000 was allocated from his will for an extravagant funeral. As the last guests departed the ceremony, his wife Mary, turned to her dearest friend.

"Well, I'm sure John would be very happy," she exclaimed.

"I'm sure he would," replied Kate, who leaned in close and whispered. "How much did this funeral cost?"

"Everything," said Mary. "$35,000."

"Wow!" Kate exclaimed. "I mean, it was amazing, but $35,000? for a funeral?"

Mary answered, "The funeral was $7,000 and I gave $1000 to the church.

Food and drinks were another $500. The balance went on the memorial stone."

Kate quickly did the math. "$26,500 for a memorial stone? how big is it?!"

"Two and a half carats."

I will always remember the last words my grandfather said to me.

"Are you holding that ladder good and tight?"

A man eating at a restaurant is so impressed with his chicken dish that he calls the waiter over.

"Excuse me, this dish is incredible. Tell me, how do you prepare the chicken?"

"Well, we give it to them straight and just tell them that they're going to die."

A woman had been in a coma for months. The Nurses were giving her a sponge bath. As one of them was washing her private parts she noticed that there was a slight response on the life support when she touched her most intimate area.

To make sure it wasn't a one off they tried it one more time and yet again there was definite movement. They called her husband and explained what happened, telling him, "As unusual as this may sound, maybe a little oral pleasure will stimulate her some more and bring her out of the coma."

The husband wasn't convinced, but the nurses promised him that they would have complete privacy. The husband eventually agreed and went into his wife's room.

After a few moments alone the woman flat lined,

no pulse, no heart rate, nothing. The nurses burst into the room back into the room and asked "What happened!?" they were shocked. The husband said, "I'm not quite sure - I suspect she may have choked."

Three mates are fishing on a boat when Jed gets up to grab a beer, he loses his balance and falls overboard. Bob says " What do we do?" Bill says, "You should jump in after him, he's been under water for a while and he's not a great swimmer." So Bob jumps in, and after a while, he surfaces with Jed. He says, "Give me a hand to get him in the boat." They eventually manage to get Jed back into the boat. Bob says, "What should we do now, he's got no pulse and he's not breathing ." Bill says, "lets do CPR, give him mouth to mouth." Bob starts to blow air into Jed's mouth and says, "Whoa, I don't remember Jed having such awful bad breath." Bill says, "that's odd, I don't think Jed was wearing a snowmobile suit either.

A guy just tried to sell me a coffin.

I said "That's the last thing I need!"

While visiting my mothers grave this morning and saw a man hiding behind a gravestone. I said, "Morning."

He replied, "No, just having a dump."

I was at my Doctors appointment when he said. "Right, I've looked over your test results and I have some good news for you" I said "wonderful, what is it"? He said "well you know you mentioned you were going to set up a pension fund"? "Yes" I said "Well don't, spend the money now" he replied

---

A doctor is talking with his patient. He says, "Would you like the good or the bad news first?"

The man replies, "The good news please."

The doctor says, "You have 24 hours to live."

"What could possibly be worse news than that?!" the man asks.

"I was trying to get hold of you yesterday."

A man is visiting his doctor surgery to get the results of his test results. The doctor asks him to take a seat as he has some rather bad news.

"You don't have long to live, I'm afraid"

"Oh, God......" he sobs, "how long do I have doc?"

"Ten....."

"Ten????!!!! Ten What? Months? Weeks? How long do I have?"

"Nine....."

A man looks over his fence and into next doors garden and sees his neighbor digging a big hole.

"Why are you digging a hole?" He asked.

"My hamster died yesterday." replied the neighbor.

"I'm terribly sorry for your loss", says the first man. "But why are you digging such a large hole?

"Well he's inside your Goddamn cat."

A couple are fighting. The wife is screaming at her husband. "I can't stand you, I want a divorce! Get out!" As he is leaving she screams: "I hope you have a slow and painful death!" The husband says: "So you want me to stay?" he says.

My neighbor was killed in an accident while overseas last week.

On a positive note, he now holds the world record for the fastest descent of Mount Everest.

Helen is grieving as her husband has just passed away. She visits the mortuary to see her beloved Alfred and upon seeing him she starts screaming hysterically.

The mortician hears the screams and rushes up to console her. While still emotional, she explains the reason she is so upset is because Alfred was wearing a black suit and he only ever wore blue suits as that was his favorite color. The mortician apologizes and explains that they always put the bodies in a black suit as standard practice, but he would see what he could do.

The next morning, Helen arrives at the mortuary to spend one last moment with her husband before his funeral. When the mortician pulls back the curtain, she manages to raise a smile as her

dear Alfred is now wearing a stunning blue suit. She asks the mortician, "Where did you get that wonderful blue suit?"

"Well, after you left yesterday, a man of a similar size to your husband was brought in wearing a blue suit. Amazingly, his wife was unhappy as she said her husband had always wanted to be buried in a black suit " the mortician replied.

He continued "And after that it was simply a matter of switching their heads around."

An old man is being interviewed on live TV

"Hello everybody. We are with James who is 96 years old. James, tell us, what's your secret"? The reporter asks.

"During the war, I gave a blowjob to a German soldier in exchange for food." James says

A shocked reported gasps "I meant the secret to looking so young".

"Oh... Eating healthy and lots of sleep" says the old man.

An attractive young woman is standing on a bridge, looking over the side and contemplating jumping.

A homeless guy approaches her.

She sees the man coming and says, "Leave me alone! You can't change my mind, I'm going to jump!"

He says, "Well, if you've definitely decided to kill yourself, let's have sex? At least I'll have a good time."

"What?! No! You pervert!", she replies. The man turns and walks away.

"Have it your way, I'll wait at the bottom, you'll still be warm."

I found my cousin hanging in the barn this morning. There was a note beside him which read, "It's all too much. I can't take the critism anymore." I gave him CPR and managed to save him in time. As he lay in my arms and slowly regained consciousness, I said, "That's not how you spell criticism."

My mother used to say the way to a mans heart is through his stomach.

Amazing woman. Terrible surgeon

What do you call a decreased magician?

Abracadava

Fred died and went to Hell. Upon arrival, the devil revealed three rooms and told him he had to choose one of them in which to spend the next 10 years.

Room one had a group of people screaming in pain while walking around on a floor of broken glass. Room 2 had a constant sound of finger nails dragging on a chalkboard that had clearly driven

everyone insane. The third room had a young attractive blonde woman giving a blowjob a fat old man.

Without hesitation Fred says, "I'll take Room 3, without a doubt."

The devil said to the woman, "OK, times up, it's Fred's turn now."

A teacher asks her pupils to tell the class what their dads do for a living.

Little Kate says: "My father is a lawyer. He puts bad people in prison."

Little Mikey says: "My Dad is a doctor. He makes all the sick people healthy again."

All the kids in the class explain what their dads do except little Jimmy. The teacher says: "Jimmy, what does your Dad do for a living?"

"My Dad is dead." Jimmy says:

"Oh dear. I'm so sorry to hear that, but what did

he do before he passed away?"

"He went, "Urrrrgghh...arrrghh...and then he crapped himself."

An old Jewish man was on his death bed and he asks for his wife to come to his bedside.

"Adah, we've been together since we were teenagers. When we were captured during the war and put into a concentration camp, you were there beside me."

"When the war ended, we moved to America, got married and had to work 12 hour days just so we could afford a tiny apartment, and you were there beside me."

"Later when my business failed and we were again left with hardly anything, you were by my side."

"And now finally, as I am about to draw my dying breath, you are there beside me"

"Adah , I'm starting to think you're are a jinx!"

I didn't sleep so well last night! I was at an old friends funeral yesterday and I caught the wreath!

I though I saw someone waving at me today but I couldn't work out if they were waving at me or someone behind me.

I'm an awful lifeguard.

When I leave this world, I want to go peacefully like my father did, in his sleep. Not screaming in panic like the passengers in his cab.

A dying old man wanted to take his life savings with him when he passed. He requested a priest, a lawyer and doctor to all come to his to his bedside.

"I'm going to give you all an envelope containing $30,000 and it is my dying wish that you each put the money in my coffin when I die so I can take all my money with me." They agreed and at the funeral they each put their envelope in the coffin.

After the funeral it all became too much for the priest and he broke down in tears and confessed that he had only put $20,000 into the envelope because he needed $10,000 to have the church alter repaired

"Well, seeing as we're all being so honest," said the doctor, "I only put $10,000 in the envelope because we needed a new $20,000 kidney dialysis machine at the hospital."

The lawyer was horrified. "I'm disgusted with the both of you," he said. "I can assure you both that when I put my envelope in the coffin, it had a check for the full amount of $30,000."

A woman asks her husband "if I died, would you move on and find someone new and maybe remarry?"

He replies "It would be very hard but yes I think eventually I would want to get married again"

"Would you live together in this house?"

"Yes. This house has so many memories for me, I could never leave"

"Would you sleep together in our bed?"

"I guess so. Our children were conceived in that bed, It's very important to me"

"Would she wear my dresses?"

"I really hadn't thought about that! You've got some beautiful outfits, it would be a shame for them to never to be worn again"

"What about my golf clubs, would she use them?"

"Absolutely not, she's left handed"

A woman loses her husband after a short illness. After some time she marries again and had 6 more children. Soon after the new husband also dies but undeterred she meets another man and they get married and this time had 5 more children. She finally died and during her funeral the priest thanked the Lord for this wonderful mother and wife, "Lord Jesus Christ, they're finally together."One mourner leaned over and quietly whispers to her friend,"Which husband do you think he's referring to?" The friend replied, "none of them, I think he means her legs."

Three men arrived the gates of heaven where they were immediately greeted by Saint Peter. "Hello gentlemen, and welcome to your final resting place. In heaven we only one rule: Never, step on a duck."

"I don't think I heard correctly. Can you say that again please?" one of the men asked.

"Throughout time, conflicting stories about heaven have arisen. Yes, sure its a wonderful

place but its not perfect, it is however pretty close. The only real issues are the ducks. If you happen to step on a duck it will begin to quack and its like a chain reaction, all the other ducks will start to quack and there isn't a moments peace. So if you step on a duck, you must accept the consequences." Saint Peter says.

The three men didn't really take too much notice and carried on into heaven. There were ducks everywhere, as far as the eye could see. Straight away one of the men accidentally stepped on a duck. As St. Peter had warned, the duck began to quack and then all the other ducks began a deafening wave of quacking.

When the quacking had finally stopped, Saint Peter approached the man who caused all the commotion, with a very unattractive old woman. Without a word, he chained the old hag and the man together and he left.

The other two men tried their best not to step on a duck but alas one of them eventually did. Saint Peter arrived again with a frightening looking woman with sores all over her face. He chained the woman to the man and left.

The final man, learning from the other mens mistakes, successfully managed to avoid stepping on any ducks. One day, Saint Peter approached

the man with a stunningly beautiful woman. He chained him and the women together and left without uttering a word.

The man could not believe his luck, "I'm speechless, whatever did I do to deserve this blessing?"

The woman responded, "I have no idea but I stood on a duck."

A man hails a cab and gets in and the driver says, "Perfect timing. You're just like Bill."

Passenger: "Who's Bill?"

Cab driver: "Bill Henderson. He's a guy who got everything right every time. Like this cab coming along just when you needed it, things like that used to happen to Bill Henderson all the time."

Passenger: "Everybody has their fair share of bad luck."

Cab driver: "Not Bill Henderson. He was an

amazing athlete. He could have won a major tennis tournaments. He could play golf with the best of the best. He sang like Pavarotti and danced like Fred Astaire and boy could he play the piano. He really was something else."

Passenger: "Sounds like he was one of a kind."

Cab driver: "That's just the beginning. He had a mind like Stephen Hawking. He never forgot anyone's birthday. He knew what wine complemented what style of food. He could turn his hand to anything. Not like me. I change a light bulb and the whole street has a blackout. But Bill Henderson just did everything right."

Passenger: "Wow, what a legend!"

Cab driver: "He always knew how to avoid traffic jams and take the most direct route to a destination. Not like me, I alway screw it up. He sure knew how to treat a lady right and make her feel special. Even if she was in the wrong he would never answer her back. He was always perfectly groomed and he dressed beautifully. He really was the perfect guy! No one could ever live up to Bill Henderson, a God amongst men."

Passenger: "How did you know him?"

Cab driver: "Well I never actually met Bill but I married his widow."

A phone rings a little girl picks it up.

"Hello?"

"Hi baby, it's daddy. Can I speak with mom, is she there?"

"She's upstairs in the bedroom with uncle Tom."

After a short silence, the father says, "But honey, you don't have an uncle Tom."

"Yes I do, he and mommy are upstairs together in the bedroom!"

After another short silence, "OK honey I want you to help me play a joke on mommy, I want you to run upstairs and shout to mommy that daddy's car just pulled up outside."

The little girl agrees and returns to the phone a few moments later.

"OK Daddy, I played the joke on mommy!"

"And what happened baby?"

"Well, mommy freaked out and jumped out of bed screaming! Then she tripped, hit her head on the wardrobe and now she isn't moving!"

"Oh Jesus!!! What about your uncle Tom?"

"He freaked out too and jumped out of bed and

then jumped out of the back window and landed in the swimming pool! I don't think he knew you drained it yesterday and now he's just lying there and he's not moving either"

After a brief pause.

"Swimming pool? Is this 555-4273?

Two women are out painting the town red on a girls night out. They get very drunk and at the end of the night they start walking home but need to make a toilet stop on the way. They relieve themselves in a cemetery but they don't have toilet paper to wipe themselves. One woman uses her panties and the other uses a wreath she finds on a grave. The next morning, one husband calls the other and says.

"That's it - no more girls nights out - Lara came home without her panties last night."

"That's nothing?" says the other husband, "Helen came home with a card stuck in her pussy that said 'we will never forget you from all the crew at the fire station."

DEAD JOKES

A man enters a brothel with only $10. He asks the madam if he can get some loving for $10. She tells him he can have the dead hooker in room 12. As he doesn't have much choice he agrees. A few minutes later he approaches the madam and says, "that was awesome but I don't think she was dead because she has a runny nose!". The madam laughs and says, "No, she's most certainly dead, it just means she's full."

My friend, Kyle died yesterday so I went to pay my respects to his wife.

Trying to be positive I said, "Look on the bright side, at least this is an end to his suffering."

She said, "He wasn't ill, he died in his sleep."

I said, "I know, I meant being married to you."

I found it really hard turning off my wife's life support earlier.

Who in their right mind would put a power point behind a wardrobe?

A dying man lying in his hospital bed begins to thrash about and make movements as if he would like to say something. A priest leans in close and gently asks, "Is there something you need to get off your chest my son?"

The man nods and the priest handed him a pen and notepad.

The priest said, "I know you are unable speak but if you would like to write it down I will give it to your wife, She's just outside."

Gathering what little strength he had, the man manages to write a few words and hands the note to the priest. Soon after, the man died.

The priest gives him the last rites and then tells his wife of his passing. After comforting her, he

gives her the note.

"These your husband's final words. He wrote them especially for you."

The distraught women reads aloud: "Get off of my oxygen hose!!"

A woman is greeted by St. Peter at the Pearly Gates. St. Peter said to her, "I see you have lived a good life and you are most welcome to pass through the gates of heaven under one condition."

The woman replied, "Sure, what's the condition"

Peter said to her, "You must spell the word: Jesus."

The woman spelled out the word, "J - E - S - U - S" and St. Peter invites her into heaven.

St. Peter had matters to discuss with the Lord and asks her to guard the gate until he returns. Peter tells the woman that anyone who wishes to enter

the gate must spell the word.

An hours passes and the womans husband appears at the gate.

She asks him "Why are you here?" .

"Well," he said, "After your funeral I was going home and I was in a fatal car accident"

The woman told him, "I see, well before you can enter the gates of heaven you must spell a word."

"Fine, what's the word?" he asked.

"Supercalifragilisticexpialidocious," she said.

After a priest dies and goes to heaven, he notices a cab driver had been awarded a higher position than him.

"I don't get it God," he moans. "I dedicated my life to the church and my parishioners."

God explains, "In heaven, we are a results driven organization. Did you offer your parishioners

engaging sermons that held their attention?"

"Sometimes," the priest admits, "the odd person fell asleep from time to time."

"That's the point," said God, "When people were in this man's cab, not only were they always awake, many of them prayed."

A man dies and goes to hell. He is told by the devil that he can choose to stay in one of three rooms for all eternity. In room one it's the classic fire and brimstone scenario where people are screaming in agony. In room two, people are being savaged by wild beasts. In room three people are standing waist-deep in shit and drinking coffee. The man realizes that none of the options are great but chooses room three. He wanders over to the coffee machine and grabs himself a cup of coffee. He's congratulating himself for making the right decision when there is an announcement over a PA system: "Attention sinners! Coffee break is over! Get back on your heads!"

Hank and Fred were serious baseball fans. They went to every game they could. They spent their entire adult lives obsessed with baseball. They made a pact that whoever died first, they would try to let the other know if there was baseball in heaven.

Hank died away in his sleep and a few nights after, Fred, awoke to the sound of Hank's voice from the grave.

"Is that you? Hank" said Fred.

"Its sure is, it's me," Fred replied.

"This is AMAZING" Fred exclaimed. "So what's the deal, can you play baseball in heaven?"

"Good news and some bad news on that front Fred. Which news you want to hear first?"

"Hit me with good news first."

"Ok, yes, you can play baseball in heaven, Fred."

"Awesome! So what's the bad news?"

"You're pitching next week."

This is the toughest part of the job," said the police officer after John was pronounced dead at the scene of the accident.

"Try and be compassionate when you break the news to his wife. She's a really sensitive lady." says his colleague.

The police officer rings the bell and Adam's wife opens the door.

The officer asks "Are you John's widow?"

A young man asked wealthy old man how he made his fortune.

"Well, son, It was during the depths of the Great Depression. I only had a nickel to my name. I took that nickel and I bought an apple. I polished the bejaysus out of that apple and I sold it for ten cents.

"The following day, I invested that ten cents and bought two apples. Again, I polished the bejaysus out of them and sold them for 20 cents.

I continued doing this for a month by which time I had made an impressive $1.37. Then my wife's father died and left us a million dollars in his will."

During a Sunday sermon torrential rain begins to fall and not long after the church starts flooding. The congregation start to exit the church but the preacher remains firm and stays in the church in the ankle-deep water.

A man in a car drives by the church and yells out, "Preacher, you better get out of there before its too late, you'll drown!"

The preacher shouts back, "Don't worry. God will save me." The the man drove off.

The rain kept falling and now the rain is knee-deep. A man passes by the church in a row boat and calls out to the preacher, "You have to leave or you will drown!" The determined preacher shouts back, "Don't worry. God will save me." The man paddles on down the flooded street.

The rain keeps coming and now the water is waist-deep and a man on a jet ski came past by the church and calls out to the preacher, "You need to leave or you will drown!" Again, the preacher declines and replies, "Don't worry. God will save me." So he jetted off.

The water has now risen to the preachers neck and he decides to climb onto the church roof. A man in a chopper flies by and calls out to the preacher, "You need to come with me or you will drown!" But the preacher stood his ground and replied, "Don't worry. God will save me." With that the chopper flies off.

The biblical rain is so intense that it covers the entire church and drowns the preacher.

When the preacher meets God in heaven he asks, "Lord, Why didn't you save me from drowning?"

God replied, "I offered you a car, a boat, a jet ski and even a chopper! I ran out of things to send!"

The priest was preparing to give a dying man the last rites.

The priest says, "Renounce Satan! Let him know good triumphs over evil!"

The dying man is silent.

Again the priest repeats his command, renounce Satan! The dying man still doesn't say a word.

The priest asked, "Why won't you reject Beelzebub and his evil?"

The dying man said, "Well I don't know where I'm going to end up so I don't want to piss anyone off!"

A man is out jogging and notices an unusual funeral procession approaching the local cemetery. Two black hearses were followed by a man walking a Rotweiler. Behind him were 100 men walking in single file.

The mans curiosity got the better of him and he approached the man with the dog "May I offer my sincerest condolences sir and ask whose funeral this is?"

"Well, my wife is in the first hearse." The man says

"Oh, what happened?"

"She was attacked by my dog." The man replied

The man was still curious, "I see, and the second hearse?"

The man replied, "My mother-in-law. She tried to stop the attack but the dog savaged her as well and she died from her injuries."

A brief silence passes between the two men.

"Do you think I could I borrow your dog?"

"You'll have to get to the end of the queue"

A man notices a friends car is absolutely trashed. The headlights are smashed and the hood is covered with leaves, grass, tree branches and blood. He asks his friend, "What the hell happened to your car?"

"I ran over a lawyer", the friend exclaims

"I see," says the man, "that explains the blood, but what about the leaves, grass and tree branches?"

"Well, I had to chase him into a park ."

A man notices a rather unsightly mole on his nose. Over time the mole gets larger and more colorful and he decides to get it checked out by a specialist. The doctor runs some tests and comes back to give the man his diagnosis, "Well, would you like the good news or the bad news first?"

"Well," give it to me straight Doc, give me the bad news first."

"The lump on your nose is a stage 4 melanoma and its already spread to your lungs, brain and other major organs and I estimate you have about 30 days to live."

"Oh sweet baby Jesus!" says the, man. "What's the good news?!"

"Well," says the doctor, "Did you happen to notice that stunning receptionist when you came in? Well, I'm sleeping with her!"

My Grandfather said to me, "The problem with your generation is that you're too reliant on technology!" I replied, "No Grandpa, your generation is too reliant on technology!" as I switched off his life support.

A gallery owner phones an artist who is displaying paintings in his gallery." Right, "I have good news and bad news," the gallery owner says. "The good news is that a guy was in today and he was admiring your artwork and wondered if they would increase in value after you died. I told him they would and he bought all of your paintings."

"That's awesome news!" the artist said. "What's the bad news?"

"Unfortunately he was your doctor."

A couples barn burns to the ground and the wife calls the insurance company.

She says, "The barn was insured for $60,000 and I want a cheque."

"I'm sorry madam but its not that straightforward. Insurance doesn't work that way. We will send out an assessor and work out the value of what was insured and provide you with a replacement of equal value."

There is silence before the wife replies, "Also, I'd like to cancel my husbands insurance policy."

Mary O'Brien is home when she hears a knock at the door, its Finbarr Murphy. "Mary, may I come in?" he asks. "I've some news to tell you."

"Yes of course you can come in but where's my husband?"

"That's what I'm here to be tell you, Mary. There was an accident down at the brewery"

"Oh, Jesus no!" cries Mary.

Seamus is dead. I'm so sorry."

She looked up at Finbarr. "What happened?"

"It was awful. He fell into a massive tank of Guinness and he drowned."

"Oh Jesus Christ. Tell me, did he die quickly?"

"Well, actually no he didn't, he got out three times to piss."

A guy sprints into a hospital, past the receptionist and towards the blood stained doctor coming out of the operating theatre.

"Doctor! Doctor!? I hear there was a terrible accident. How is my wife doing?"

"I'm so sorry, she's been horrifically burned and she has a severe brain injury. You will probably have to feed her as she's paralyzed. You'll need to take her to the toilet and wipe her afterwards. You will also have to bathe her. I'm sorry I know this is a lot to take in but I'm afraid there is more. Your insurance won't cover this. Your are going to have to pay for her medication and other costs out of your own pocket. She is going to need care round the clock and she could live a very long time.

The husband is so shocked that he is unable to speak. He just stands there dazed with tears in his eyes.

Finally, the doctor says, "Hah, you should see your face. I'm just messing with you. She's dead."

A 70 year-old woman was visited by the Lord himself and he told her that she has another 40 years before her time was up".

The woman was ecstatic and vowed to make the most of the next 40 years!

She immediately went out and had some very intensive plastic surgery including liposuction, a boob job, nose job, a face lift - the works.

She went to a beauty parlor and had her hair and face done by a professional make up artist. When she left the beauty parlor she crossed the street to buy some new clothes and she was hit by a speeding truck and killed instantly..

She met with God at the pearly gates and angrily said, "What's the deal Lord?!!!! You said I had 40 years left"

God looked at her closely and said "Opps, me bad! I didn't recognize you!"

Printed in Great
Britain
by Amazon